LESSONS LEARNT

SIBUSISO KUMALO

Copyright © SIBUSISO KUMALO
All rights reserved. No part of this book may be used or reproduced in any manner whatsoever without written permission except in the case of brief quotations embodied in critical articles or reviews.

Published in the year 2021 by
MFH PUBLISHERS
A division of Mathebe Family Holdings (PTY) LTD
For information contact:
Email: Info@MFHpublishers.co.za
Www.MFHpublishers.co.za

ISBN 978-0-620-94515-8
Cover design and editing
by MFH Publishers

DEDICATION

To all the voices unheard,
I dedicate this book to you.

Contents

Dedication..iii
CHAPTER ONE..
CHAPTER TWO 1
CHAPTER THREE... 15
CHAPTER FOUR... 35
CHAPTER FIVE... 47
CHAPTER SIX... 61
CHAPTER SEVEN... 71
CHAPTER EIGHT 79
ABOUT THE AUTHOR 95

CHAPTER ONE

"I decided that no matter what happens I will keep moving and never look back."

"Lessons learned the hard way stay
with you for a lifetime."

"I have learned not to waste my energy on
things that don't matter."

"Life is precious, that's all we need to know."

"Lies are common, the truth is rare."

"Time is a precious commodity,
I can't believe how much of it we waste."

"Never give up on making something of your life,
you have nothing to lose."

"There is nothing wrong with love,
people just take advantage."

"Advice is good unless it comes from people who
think they are better than you."

"Listening is good, it depends on
what you want to take in."

"Trust is hard to find, even harder to
keep once you find it."

"Making the right decision takes heart,
courage, and strength."

"I laugh because it is good for my soul
not because I want to act happy."

"There is no substitute for peace of mind"

"Just because I don't broadcast my problems
doesn't mean I am living a nice life."

"Once the pain goes away, I never subject
myself to the same mistake again."

"You don't care about me but you are always
on my case as if you know me."

"People think you live your life to prove a point to
them, who has the energy to do that?"

"Even if you think I am stupid,
I am not trying to prove I am smart anyway."

"I have learned some harsh lessons,
mistakes I promise never to make again."

"Advice is good unless it comes from people
who think they are better than you."

"Beautiful people are hard to find,
just like honest people."

"Loyalty is rare, just like honesty"

"People have no loyalty."

"Some people are all about talk and no action."

"People like throwing insults,
it still doesn't make you a better person."

"I suffer alone and in silence,
then you think my life is a smooth ride."

"Loving someone isn't the problem,
being loved back is."

"I don't live my life based on
what you think is right for me."

"You have achieved what you wanted,
now please leave me alone."

"You do your best to make me feel
worthless so you can feel important."

"You treat me like I am not human then you
expect me to treat you like an angel?"

"I have tried my best not to be selfish but
the world makes me think otherwise."

"Pain is a transmitted disease."

"People judge without even knowing the truth."

"Love is scarce when you
need it the most."

"Nobody cares about my pain
but they hate my happiness."

"Family is important until you are
no longer important to them."

"Trusting a person is like risking money
you will never get back."

"Some people like talking nonsense about
me as if I live my life to please them."

"I am who I am because of what I have been through."

"Worrying about someone who doesn't worry about
you is a waste of precious time that you will never get back"

"People only care about themselves but they
complain when someone doesn't care about them."

"People always love with their words but their
actions speak a different language."

"People deny the truth and
then act like I am crazy."

"Honesty doesn't exist in the world,
people only care about being right."

"Life is not a fairytale, that's why you
don't always get what you want."

"Having friends is good for a person,
having true friends is a total blessing."

"I miss being young, back then life was
full of fun with no issues."

"I don't regret any decision that I make because
at the time it was the right decision."

"I am happy to be myself, happy to be the person that I am."

"The pressures of life are too stressful.
I find it weird that people
also want to hurt other people."

"I am surprised to realize that people only notice
I am important when I am dead."

"Growing up was fun,
I don't remember anyone hating me."

"My actions define who I am,
my words define what I believe."

"My life has been defined by the obstacles
I have faced and overcome."

"Money doesn't define a person,
how he gets the money does."

"Time keeps moving, whether you are happy or sad.
So make the best out of it."

"Spend time doing the things
that make you happy."

"I have learned that people who don't
know you have a lot to say about you."

"I have grown up, not my body
but my mind, spirit and soul."

"Nobody in life wants you to have peace of mind."

"Happiness doesn't exist in the world,
you have to create your own."

"We claim to love each other but we
don't care when others are suffering."

"I have learned to accept
things I cannot change."

"There is no human being that
can bring me happiness."

"I will never impress anybody because
I don't live my life for people."

"I am not happy because
I chose not to be."

"We do nothing and then we
complain about being broke."

"Whether you are good at something or not,
hard work always pays off."

"Being a nobody is easy,
just sit around and do nothing."

"Achieving success is good, at least you have
something to console yourself with when life is not so good."

"Patience is hard work that pays off."

"Pleasing everyone is a problem that
you will never solve."

"Being myself is easier than trying
to be someone else."

"People never praise you for the effort,
they always look for mistakes."

"People don't care about you unless
you have money."

"People want to be accepted for who they are but they never
accept other people for who they are."

"Being myself makes people
criticize and dislike me,
who should I be then?"

"I miss being young and playing sports,
it was more fun than being
old and judged all the time."

"Being angry is good for a person,
afterward you let go of the frustration."

"I don't understand why some people
want to see other people
dead, that won't make them successful in life."

"People only like me because I have money."

"I wouldn't be this short or this hurt,
what did I ever do to these people?"

"I tried so hard and I still got nothing."

"Being black is a curse,
we enjoy destroying each other."

"Words make me feel unforgettable pain,
if you hate me then why you are in my business.
Leave me alone."

"There is nothing like money,
it makes people do what you want."

"Trusting people is a risk,
just ask those with broken hearts."

"If I knew there would be so much hate,
I would have chosen to be unborn."

"People are so rude, for no reason at all."

"I am allergic to pretense, it gets me nowhere."

"You cannot force anybody to like you,
let alone love you."

"Rain makes you appreciate nature,
it reminds you that you are human."

"Some fresh air relaxes the mind, body and soul."

"Effort shows you believe you can do it."

"Life is a working progress,
no matter how small the progression is."

"Always work towards a certain goal,
that way you can smile back at your achievements."

"Hard work pays off one day,
I just don't know when."

"Issues complicate every situation."

"Truth be told,
life is not fair to anyone."

"It's funny how people judge you as
if that makes them better people."

"Whether my habits are good or bad,
you are not the judge."

"My thoughts reveal the true me,
my words just deceive."

"I am honestly shy but life makes you
do unthinkable things."

"People say I have trust issues,
that's because they never gave me a
reason to trust them."

"I trust nobody and people always
prove why I shouldn't."

"Trust is a sensitive thing,

always given to the wrong people."

"Human beings always break your trust and act surprised
when you don't trust them anymore."

"I hope my children learn that respect is important,
it avoids fights and issues."

"Respect, honesty and trust helps people to
keep their friends closer."

"Being respected brings a lot of
comfort to one's heart."

"Being smart always helps, you make good decisions
no matter what the situation is."

"People claim you are nothing,
it's funny they don't say that when they need your help."

"People laugh at your pain and misfortune then
they claim *"umuntu umuntu ngabantu"*

"People get disgusted at my sight,
I wonder what I ever did to them."

"I woke up this morning, I am grateful."

"I try my best to avoid issues but people
always bring them into my life."

"Judging me won't make
you a better person."

"Sacrificing is a great thing to do
because you don't get praised for it."

"People don't support you but
expect to be part of your success."

"Peace of mind is a blessing because
the world always brings problems your way."

"I can walk, talk, run and do things for myself.
Bless everyone who is disabled."

"My humble beginnings made me who I am today."

"I wish joy to every human being so we
can all be happy."

"Thoughts reflect my true self, I can be me without

any judgment in my thoughts."

"Everybody pretends as if they like me and they talk shit about me behind my back."

"I choose to ignore people who act better at my expense."

"Some people act like they are better than me when they haven't achieved half the things I have achieved."

"There are a lot of things I wish I could have done, guess time waits for no one."

"Some people act like life revolves around them, why don't you die and let's see."

"African football is improving, that's how life should be at all times."

"I chose to ignore some people, all they know is talking about other people."

"I can't change the fact that I am from the dusty streets of Soweto, that's why I am who I am today."

"Perfection doesn't exist but some people act like they are perfect."

"Follow your heart, your mind will tell you if it's the correct decision or not."

"My fears don't define me; they show that some things are not worth taking the risk for."

"Favoritism causes issues at every place."

"If you are happy inside, nobody can take that away from you."

"Follow your instinct because it advises you about what is right not what people tell you."

"Struggle has made me stronger than I was before"

"Pain is not the end, it's the reason to move on."

"Truth relieves the burden and frees the soul."

"Discussions opens the mind,

arguments damage the mind."

"Being hurt by someone you know is more
painful than someone you don't know."

"The possibilities are endless,
it's too bad we are too blind to see them."

"Life just passed me by,
what happened."

"Keeping things simple makes you the best."

"Even if you don't like someone,
respect goes a long way in avoiding issues."

"Loyalty is rare to find,
let alone keep."

"Honesty helps you to rectify
your mistakes and flaws."

"Progress comforts me,
I know I am heading the right way."

"Hunger for success will make you successful."

"People use you and treat you like
a piece of shit afterward."

"Pain makes you cruel."

"I guess it took me a long time to figure
out that I never had a family."

"Love doesn't exist in my life, just hatred."

"No trust in my heart and I know why."

"The truth is all I need to save my soul"

"A smile makes you believe all kinds of lies."

"Peace brings happiness to the soul."

"As I grow older I grow wiser and rectify all my mistakes,
making sure they never happen again."

"Inspiration comes from the words of wisdom"

"True love doesn't exist,
only conditional love."

"My heart longs for love yet the
universe serves plenty of pain."

"Humility is the realization
that we are all human."

"Living your life is a blessing no one
can take away from you."

"Depending on people is like
trusting the devil."

"Pain makes you realize some people
never cared in the first place."

"Impressing people takes you nowhere in life,
wait till you have a problem."

"I try to be a better person every day."

"If you think you have real friends,
just wait till you need help to find out the truth."

"My mind grows wiser every day,
I hope I make good decisions in the future."

"Every day is another chance to
improve on life in general."

"If something doesn't work,
you can always try something else."

"The journey to my dreams is
bumpy but I will get there."

"All the sacrifices you make will be
in vain if it's for ungrateful people."

"You can compromise a thousand times
but nobody will compromise for you."

"Difficult decisions are
the ones that mean progress."

"Take a journey towards happiness,
no matter how many obstacles you come across,
just know you are on the right path."

"Life is an art we will never master
because it is unpredictable."

"I guess my life experiences have
made me who I am today."

"I don't see any reason to be jealous,
be inspired to achieve as well."

"People criticize other people
instead of living their lives."

"It's hard to believe I made it this far after
all the torture I have been through"

"The truth will not change no matter
how many times you lie."

"We turn a blind eye to the truth,
that's why we don't progress."

"Even if you can boast to people,
they don't care."

"The only way people will like you is if you do
what they want and that won't happen."

"I cannot change my past,
I can learn from it."

"I am honest with myself so that I can improve
the person that I am."

"People suffer for the truth."

"Living in fear is the same as not living at all."

"We always want things that are far away from
us because we are craving the spotlight."

"Life is not entirely hard, it is just issues
being created by heartless people."

"Black people celebrate failure, embrace the
death of another black person."

"My pain is enjoyed by many people,
who are constantly against me."

"People hate my existence and despise my progress."

"The true colors of a person are reflected when they

are confronted by the truth."

"Your curses and trash talk won't change who I am."

"You can insult me a million times,
my success will hurt more than all your insults."

"With all due respect, I don't live my life for you."
"Being positive makes your task easier to achieve."

"I am amazed by the nasty comments thrown at me,
I didn't ask for anybody's opinion."

"I have learned that knowledge without ambition
and focus takes you nowhere."

"Don't analyze who I am or what I do,
it's none of your business."

"My search for peace and tranquility
starts in my heart."

"Good people help you when
you least expected."

"We get surprised when we get help
from black people, I wonder why."

"Dedication, commitment and hard work go hand in hand.
You cannot achieve success without all three."

"I don't always do the right thing,
just the simple things that works."

CHAPTER TWO

"If you can hold my hand through hard times,
I will hold your hand through difficult times as well."

"Compromise makes it easy to reach your goals."

"I have grown up to realize some people get
disgusted at my happiness."

"Perfection is impossible, so why are we
judging each other."

"I am not perfect, I am human just like all of you."

"If it was up to me I would always be happy
but reality doesn't agree."

"Having someone hold your hand during
hard times is truly a blessing."

"Knowledge is good for the world but people prefer knowing
nothing and claiming they are streetwise."

"To find peace, I have to search within myself."

"Money doesn't change a person, the person decides to
change because they have money."

"Money is not the devil, it is a way to survive in today's world."

"Black people only criticize and bring down other black
people but they still think they will reach the promised land."

"I enjoy today, dream about tomorrow,
and cherish yesterday's memories."

"Assumptions lead to people making the wrong decisions."

"Sharing your knowledge is the best thing you can do,
that's how you get more
understanding in the first place."

"People don't want to compromise,
that's why there is so much pain in the world."

"Don't compare yourself with anybody,
you have no idea how difficult their life is."

"I long for the day people will love other
people for who they are."

"When we all work together things work out but some people
want to be successful by themselves."

"The beauty of hard work is in the reward"

"Life continues even though
many people don't like you,
it's not like you are living your life for them anyway."

"A gesture of any sort is a sign of true respect."

"If you have a talent, use it,
that's your only way of being successful."

"Kindness is always taken for a weakness,
then we complain when people are unkind."

"If you do something to prove a point,
you forget the main reason you are doing it in the first place."

"If you think success comes easy
then you are still living in dreamland."

"Learn as much as you can,
it is always beneficial."

"I am amazed by so much energy being put into hatred,
you gain nothing from it."

"Having a good time is good,
it relaxes the mind and releases stress."

"If you are not a favorite in the world, life won't be easy."

"Perseverance pays off in the end,
at the time when we least expected."

"Life will be a long, hard road if you pretend to
be someone else."

"Experiences create memories that last forever."

"Working towards something motivates you
than working towards nothing."

"Hatred is unnecessary,
pain and stress being put on your heart."

"Being scared to face reality is like living in a dream."

"Poverty is a reason to reach for your dreams."

"Success is a foreign word where I come from,
all we know is poverty."

"Being black, our best talent is bringing each other down."

"Insults are part of black people,
we take pride in insulting each other."

"People call me all sorts of names
but they know my real name."

"It's hard to find true friends,
they are the ones who hurt us the most."

"My soul has been tortured by the world,
just because I refused to give it up for the world."

"Sometimes in life we overthink, just do it."

"Time moves quickly, make the most of it."

"Knowledge is a weapon you can
use to fight poverty."

"For you to understood, you have to go through it."

"If you have a good work ethic, you always get rewarded."

"Denying the truth and lying to yourself
will lead to the same mistakes."

"Being responsible is a choice you make so that you
can do all the important things in life."

"Claiming that you are a matured person
doesn't make you matured."

"Joy is a great feeling because of pain."

"A true sense of achievement is when
you see your dreams coming true."

"Pushing boundaries always takes you to the next level."

"Being in control of a situation
makes it easy to deal with."

"When anger and hatred takes over your heart,
you forget the true purpose of
why we are here on earth."

"Anger management is good
but letting off steam is
better than keeping it bottled up."

"Problems come at the wrong time,
all we can do is wait for the right
time for them to go away."

"We all have a brain, some decide to
use it and some don't."

"The greatest joy in life is being appreciated for
who you are and what you have done"

"Inspiration pushes you to greater heights."

"If we work without issues we achieve
unlimited success."

"Just focus on your goals and they
will become a reality."

"When I feel down I just think about the good times
and put a smile on my face."

"Inspiration comes from true events that
we need to learn from."

"Making the right choice takes guts because it
doesn't benefit everybody."

"True sacrifices are made for family, some appreciate it
and some throw it back in your face."

"We are all talented at something,
the important thing is realizing what is it."

"We can't all be good at one thing,
everybody has their own field of expertise."

"Money is a universal language that we
should all learn to speak."

"True friends want to see you happy,
fake friends find a way to make you cry."

"My true self comes out when I am by myself
because the world is too judge mental."

"We all have our own beliefs,
then why is it hard to accept each other."

"Sacrifice and hard work takes you places
but we want things to come easy."

"Education is not a guarantee that you will be

successful but it's better than nothing."

"Don't hesitate to follow your dreams,
when they come true you won't regret it."

"My attitude towards life pushes me to reach
bigger things despite people's insults."

"The extra effort always counts otherwise you will be
just another average person"

"A life lived with fewer issues brings more happiness,
success and tranquility."

"Talking about it is an idea,
doing it is a recipe for success."

"Put 100% into everything you do,
the rewards will be beyond your wildest dreams."

"I am encouraged to improve my life everyday,
I don't see any reason why not."

"The world is full of selfish people who would rather see
you die than to compromise."

"A life full of issues is a life wasted."

"Anything easy to do is boring because you
already know what is going to happen."

"An opportunity must be used because there is
no guarantee of a second chance"

"Telling yourself that you will do it next time means you are
staying in the same place and not progressing"

"Moving on with life doesn't mean forgetting
where you come
from because that's what made you who you are."

"A challenge is a chance to learn something,
something to expand your knowledge."

"Sacrificing yourself for the good of
mankind is truly gracious."

"Trust has never been a bad thing, people just misuse it."

"The person you trust is the one that breaks your trust
without caring and they act like everything is okay."

"Sometimes what is important doesn't benefit you,
it benefits everyone around you."

"No matter how many times you try to deal with death,
it's always shocking"

"The same people that say they are your friends are
the same people that throw insults at you
behind your back"

"I am not a perfect person,
that's why I try to improve every day."

"Nothing brings pure joy than to be loved and cherished."

"True blessings have nothing to do with money"

"I never felt stupid because people called me stupid and
I never felt stupid because people
disrespected me."

"People always try to make me feel useless, I wonder why"

"I never compare myself to anyone, I live my own life."

"People have opinions about me that
I have never asked for."

"Some people forget about you when life isn't going well,
they remember you when their
lives are not going well."

"People who tell you that you can't do something,
they can't do it either."

"People suddenly care about you when you die"

"My mind is way beyond society's ways of living."

"Beauty doesn't fascinate me because I have learned that
people are only beautiful outside"

"Degrading comments are the pride and joy
of black people."

"Progress is something that we should all strive for otherwise
we will stay in the same place."

"True respect is shown by people you don't know."

"My character is a true reflection of who I am"

"Trusting humans is like asking a
lawyer not to lie."

"The beauty of silence is the tranquility and peace."

"Inspirational stories touch my soul, they make me believe that
I can make it no matter what"

"Having a different mentality to society
makes you an outcast."

"Freedom is beautiful because nothing is forced on you."

"Victory is not when I get money but when I
overcome all my obstacles."

"A matured mind thinks about the
wellbeing of all mankind."

"Music brings peace to my heart that no
human being will ever bring."

"People only do what suits them,
they don't care about anybody else."

"People always do what they think instead of the
simple things, that's what life is about."

"True legends are not judged by their
achievements but by their humility."

"Life's events leave me speechless."

"Through hard times do we realize our strength"

CHAPTER THREE

"Beauty that shines from inside to the outside is truly a precious gift."

"Patience is the reason some people are successful"

"It hurts till it doesn't hurt anymore then
the heart turns cold."

"My dreams will be fulfilled once I see all the
people in the world happy."

"Peace is the symbol of love, care and serenity.
I pray for its existence to last forever."

"Patience is the key to true success,
without it you go nowhere."

"One opportunity taken opens more opportunities."

"Doing nothing makes me feel weird,
it feels like I am applying for failure."

"Living the life you want brings joy,
peace and happiness."

"People always let you down,
the key is never expecting too much."

"I am blessed to be who I am, some people are less
privileged than I am. I am forever grateful."

"Put yourself in another person's shoes and you will
understand why life is so cruel at times."

"Life has hardships that no man can predict
but that everyman can conquer."

"Self-realization is a blessing because you
start being the true you."

"Moving forward is a state of mind, you have to see
progress in your mind first before
it becomes reality."

"I admire people of all races and cultures because
that's what respect is all about."

"Truth doesn't exist, they all pretend as
long as it suits them."

"The hatred gets served to me by everybody,
I am not surprised."

"People always assume they know it all,

I wonder what makes you so sure."

"Don't act like you like me when I am dead
because it means nothing."

"Black minds will never grow and realize
the truth of the world."

"Petty arguments don't grow the mind."

"Some people think life is full of hand-outs."

"People treat you like a nobody
when you don't have money."

"Some things never change,
stupid people just grow to be more of themselves."

"I will never change who I am even
though you hate me."

"Talking about useless people is a
waste of precious time."

"As I am growing old I realize some people never wanted
to see me happy ever since I was born."

"The truth is what makes me who I am spiritually and
emotionally because I realize the facts of life."

"The heart is sensitive and fragile,
I would rather give it to a dog than a human being."

"Peace and love is what we should all strive for in life
then we will see a happy nation of people."

"I have learned hard lessons but I
don't regret any decision I have made."

"I walk my road, live my reality,
speak my thoughts, feel my emotions."

"Pain is temporary but love is permanent
and it brings everlasting joy."

"Living an ordinary life is what black people strive
for and those black people hate black people
who achieve extraordinary things."

"Some people never want to see a black person smile,
they only want tears and suffering."

"I am reaching for the sky, reaching for my full potential, that's what life is all about, 100% or nothing."

"Children are good people, in a sense that they don't destroy anybody's life."

"Lies are the reason for heartache and sorrow yet we live our lives behind a bunch them."

"The start and finish might be the same, it's who you are in the middle that matters."

"I am driven by the desire to make it, desire to live life to the fullest."

"Rather speak and be heard than die and be forgotten."

"I take it one day at a time because life is about treasuring the finer moments."

"Our human nature makes us one being."

"What is the purpose of love with no trust and respect?."

"Respect is a big symbol of pure love."

"The sense of progression is the improvement of your mindset."

"Being broke doesn't define who you are but staying broke does."

"A sense of purpose is a driving force to do what you were put on earth to do."

"A true sense of belonging brings peace into your heart."

"People create rumors about you and then they say you have issues."

"Simple things always work."

"Trust people at your own risk."

"True friends are rare, they are hidden behind fake friends."

"Treat each other with love and care and see

how happy both of you will be."

"Take care of each other's feelings and
you will find true happiness."

"No matter what situation I am in,
a positive spirit always pulls me through."

"Just focus on your gift and you will
do wonders and even surprise yourself."

"Put your work first and
you will grow to be a legend."

"Appreciation is a true reflection of being humble."
"Support is vital in a man's success."

"The more you depend on people, the more
disappointment you will endure."

"The true purpose of knowledge is the success gained."

"It's important to be grateful so that you can be
blessed more than you are already."

"Ubuntu is shown to people who didn't
expect it, that's the beauty of it."

"My life is a reflection of my experiences."

"I appreciate everybody who has
ever helped me in any way."

"Through patience, I have learned so
much and survived hard times."

"Love is what you give and you are blessed to get it back."

"A true genius never shows off."

"Success is the result of pure perseverance
through all circumstances."

"The life of a hero is not based on what he does to gain
popularity but what he does when nobody is looking."

"I am a dreamer and I will continue to dream
until there is peace in the world."

"It's easy to walk through a storm hand in hand."

"In the world, you are always remembered for

your work, not anything else."

"In black culture, all the so-called stupid people are rich
and the so-called smart people have nothing."

"A sincere heart always loves no matter
how great the pain is."

"Being different is hard, people always treat
you in a certain manner."

"Truly time has passed,
I can't even recognize myself anymore."

"The beauty of success is the patience
it took to get there."

"The demons inside me put my beliefs to the
ultimate test which I will always pass."

"Sometimes thinking too much makes
your dreams pass you by."

"I have learned that being stubborn
takes you nowhere."

"Peace in my heart is vital, that's where world peace begins."

"To all black people: No matter how much you know English,
you are still black."

"If you know your culture then you are a true African."

"Some people are nice and kind,
despite all the evil in the world."

"Being discouraged makes me
more eager to succeed."

"Criticizing me brings the best out of me."

"One of the hardest things in life is swallowing your pain
and be happy to see someone you love, loving someone else."

"Someone inspires me to be myself, thank you"

"I don't do any favors, I go all out and leave no regrets."

"Black people think they are smart because
they drink alcohol,
I wonder what you ever achieved by doing that."

"It's funny how many insults black people
throw at you and
then they expect you to give back to the community."

"The truth is just the truth, it has
nothing to do with proving a point."

"Sometimes we do the same thing over and over
again and we think we are smart."

"Faith makes things happen,
hope is waiting for fate to be decided."

"Arguing with people who can't admit
the truth is a waste of time."

"I have grown to realize some people act matured
but they are more foolish than before"

"Your insults won't destroy me,
they will make me better than I am today."

"Caring about people that don't care
about you is the most painful thing."

"Everything makes sense with time."

"Things are better off done by yourself."

"Let poverty turn you into a hustler for life."

"Patience is the key to all great things."

"I have grown to realize that
everything happens for a reason."

"There is no turning back,
only moving forward."

"Some people think you are stupid
because you are not like them."

"Life is full of surprises so fewer
expectations are better."

"Silence helps me through a lot of difficulties."

"Patience is hard, harder than we think."

"I have never let discouraging comments
bring my spirit down."

"So many times I have done well without the
support I craved from people."

"I have been told to give up on my
dreams but my success
reminds me that opinions don't matter, only results."

"People are remembered for the good work they
have done in the world and nothing else."

"Throughout all difficulties humanity still stands."

"Don't look back, you have already moved on."

"I believe whatever happens was meant to
happen regardless of what people think."

"Regardless of all my circumstances,
I am inspired to do good all the time."

"Opinions don't change the facts."

"Knowledge allows you to make the right
decisions at the right time."

"Nobody knows your destiny so the
insults won't decide your fate"

"Everyone has an opinion about your life,
it still doesn't mean they are right."

"I kept going although I had no one to hold on to."

"I was told I was nothing, so I have nothing to lose when
I go after my dreams because I have nothing to lose."

"Nobody believed in me,
I made it anyway, oh well."

"Inspiration to make it comes
from being overlooked."

"Hurtful words only affect me but never
will they bring me down."

"People disrespect and
hate you for no reason"

"Children always have a smile on their faces,
true happiness."

"Don't miss any opportunity to be happy,
it might be the last."

"Sadness is the reason we all
appreciate joy so much."

"I am stronger today because of
all that I have been through."

"My understanding is that being yourself
makes you more happy
and content than pretending to be something you are not."

"I am happy to be alive today,
grateful to be blessed beyond my imagination."

"Kindness always comes from a good heart,
thank you for being a caring person."

"The people who know the least
about you are always judgmental."

"There is too much hatred and disrespect
in the world, I wonder why."

"Don't let the insults get the best of you."

"It is always a challenge to achieve more,
that is my only ambition."

"Never rest on your laurels,
you never what tomorrow has in store."

"I am blessed to be me, no matter
how hard it gets sometimes."

"Life is a big challenge that we must
never run away from."

"I am encouraged to be and do
better all the time."

"I always take the opportunity to better myself
and improve my skills all the time."

"I look back on lessons that I have learned and realized
I was meant to be who I am today."

"True humility has nothing to do
with doing any favors."

CHAPTER FOUR

"A sense of belonging brings peace
and tranquility."

"Arguing without knowing the facts is a
waste of your time and energy"

"We are all quick to jump to conclusions,
slow to give praise."

"Doing my best in everything that I do is
what I believe in"

"Hunger for knowledge will
take you places"

"My focus is on making myself better not
degrading other people."

"There is no time for hatred because we
have limited time on earth."

"No regrets, all that was done was
for a solution to be found."

"Time is important,
you won't get it back if it is wasted."

"Where I come from, time just flies without
having done anything with our lives."

"Don't place all your eggs in one basket,
they might all be broken."

"Some friends will be more loyal to you
than your actual family."

"A guy will be more loyal to you than a
woman ever will be."

"It is hard to admit the truth but it is
better than losing yourself."

"All I do now is make my life better
for me and my family."

"I am open to new ideas and ways of doing things,
that is the only way we grow."

"I am blessed to be where I am."

"Thinking out of the box helps
your mind grow"

"So many people told me I would amount
to nothing, oh well."

"I grew up to be everything I ever wanted to be,
that is all I am grateful for."

"Despite all the judgments and hypocrisy,
I am still here."

"No one can predict the future or your destiny."

"All that matters is where we finish."

"All words that come from honesty
and humility are good."

"All my obstacles, my challenges,
are the reason I am who I am today."

"I dream of one day being a good person,
not a popular person."

"Looking back, there is nothing
I would change."

"Trying to impress the world is a human disease
that only your spirit can cure."

"Dedicated, committed, ambitious, that is me"

"The greatest wish we all have is to be happy."

"My life is a reflection of who I was,
who I am, and who I want to be."

"We all have dreams, whether they
become reality or not, it's all up to you."

"Sometimes you have to go all the way to see your
dreams become a reality, you have no choice."

"Compromise is the hardest thing to do but after
it is done you will realize it was worth it."

"All my mistakes are the reason I
do my best all the time."

"All I have learned is that you can never
go wrong with hard work."

"Opportunities have passed me by, that's why I will never
let another one slip through my hands."

"I am happy to do the right thing, not because
I want attention but because it's progress."

"Today is the day I will do something about my life,
yesterday is gone and tomorrow
is not promised."

"Making a mistake is normal,
some people judge you like they are perfect."

"Never take for granted the joy you experience,
it never lasts long."

"Mistakes are part of my life,
I am constantly trying to learn from them."

"There is no point in impressing people,
they don't care anyway."

"I put so much effort into all that I do,
whether it works out or not I have no regrets."

"Don't take for granted the love you have,
it might not be there tomorrow"

"Nobody knows your destiny or your fate,
don't listen to opinions."

"Popularity won't help you to leave a good
legacy for your family."

"Whether I am mature or not,
all that matters is doing what is right."

"Make sure all good advice
stays with you forever."

"All good thoughts are good
for your health."

"Your health is more important,
so treat yourself well."

"Give yourself a chance to make
something great of your life."

"Hurting other people will
never make you happy."

"Concentrate on what matters in your life."

"I have compromised who I am many times and still got no happiness in impressing other people."

"I am never against acquiring knowledge, that is the way forward."

"Even if people talk bad things about you, they can't take away your talent or your happiness."

"I do what makes me happy, that's all that I need to do."

"Happiness is more important than anything else in this life because if you are happy then you will have peace in your heart."

"Probably the best form of love is loyalty."

"Never turn your back on a friend, they will be there when your girlfriend/boyfriend leaves."

"Today is more important than yesterday because I am living in the present and not in the past."

"The future is something we can build and not hope for."

"Do things because you want to not because you want to prove a point."

"My existence has a specific reason, I hope I will understand it properly one day."

"I work towards doing what is right not what I think is right."

"Together we are looking at a bright future, divided we will never see that bright future."

"My looks don't determine who I am inside."

"It is possible for all of us to live our dreams."

"I truly believe all that happens was meant to be, there is no mistake."

"Whether people think you are smart or stupid, your talent is all that matters."

"The desire to do good things
inspires me to keep going."

"As long as I keep pushing,
never looking back"

"Yesterday was horrific, today is better,
I will make sure tomorrow is great."

"I have come so far in life,
I cannot believe how I have been blessed."

"So many times I lost my way,
humility brought me back to the right path."

"One opportunity taken can
change your life forever."

"I don't do anything to please the public."

"I am too lost in myself to worry
about pleasing people."

"Time flies, so fly with it,
don't get left behind."

"You only realize when you are grown up
that your actions affect a lot of people."

"Maturity: when you do what is
right instead of what you want."

"I am teaching myself to always say nice things even when I am hurting."

"I became the person that I am today
because of how I grew up."

"As you grow up you outgrow some things but you always look
back and see how far you have come."

"As much as tomorrow is not promised,
you still have to look forward to it."

"Help always comes when you least expected"

"Yesterday made you stronger for today,
just like today will make you a better person for tomorrow."

"Never be in a rush to reach the promised
land because you might never get there"

"All things are possible."

"Today is another opportunity to make life
better than it was yesterday."

"I live my life as best as I can,
not as you want me too."

"No matter how long it takes,
dreams do come true one day."

"Challenging all the limits is a challenge
I am willing to take."

"Moving forward is a must not a choice."

"Humility reminds you that
you are just human."

"No support gives you more
motivation to succeed."

"Throughout my life, I have faced many obstacles
and challenges but I am still here."

"There is so much hatred, disrespect, and disregard in the world,
I wonder what we think we will gain by that."

"Inspiration comes from all the
challenges we face."

"I always look forward to a better tomorrow
no matter how bad today is."

"Positivity is the only way to get a
project done properly."

"Move past all the insults, disrespect, being belittled and you
will see that life is bigger than
negative people."

"Thinking too much makes me
make the wrong decisions,
I just need to do things"

"Improvement comes day by day,
progress is necessary."

"No matter how long it takes,
dreams do come true one day."

"I live my life as best as I can,

not as you want me to"

"Today is another opportunity to make
life better than it was yesterday."

"Yesterday made you stronger for today, just like today
will make you a better person for tomorrow."

"Help always comes when
you least expected"

"As much as tomorrow is not promised,
you still have to look forward to it."

"As you grow up you outgrow some things but you
always look back and see
how far you have come."

"I became the person that I am today
because of how I grew up."

"I am teaching myself to always say nice
things even when I am hurting."

"You only realize when you are grown that
your actions affect a lot of people."

"I have grown up, Things have changed but
I am happy to be where I am today."

"I never give up, I would rather fail
than sit and do nothing."

"No matter how hard the circumstances are,
keep your spirit burning."

"True love doesn't exist unless
there is loyalty and trust."

"I will never let my background
determine my future."

"Freedom is not being able to do what you want, it is living y
our life without being worried
about what others have to say."

"My success doesn't depend
on what you think."

"People are too focused on things that have nothing to
do with them while their

homes are falling apart."

"My happiness is not about
making you happy."

"Day to day, I am happy with my progress."

"Pain has pushed my strength to the limit
but my Strength always wins."

"My courage has brought me where I am today,
it will continue to elevate me to higher places."

"Don't ever forget who helped you to be successful,
you can repay them by helping someone else."

"Patience is everything, you cannot be
successful without it."

"Read a book, you will be knowledgeable:
I was taught."

"Study your history as a black person,
you will truly know who you are."

"I am color blind, I only see
human beings."

"Throughout my journey, I have learned that humility
is scarce but a great asset to have."

"Despite people being disrespectful and always
throwing insults, I am still myself."

"Your intelligence is not proved by your English accent,
it is proved by your
achievements and humility."

"Love doesn't exist in the world anymore,
people are only interested
if you have money to spend on them."

"There is no amount of money that can
replace peace of mind."

"Reliable people are hard to find, when you do find one.
Take care of them so that they don't leave."

"Be committed if you want to
make it, no holding back."

"Do whatever it takes to make it,

just don't cross the line."

"Effort never goes without a
ny reward."

"No matter how far I go I will never
forget where I came from."

"I am not sure how long I will live but
I will cherish every moment that I am here."

"Despite all the hardships,
my will drives me towards a better life."

"My success will not be determined
by your doubts or insults."

"Make your way forward,
it's better than going backwards."

"Keep on improving, there is no
progress in staying in one place."

"Life is a long journey, t
ake your time to make the right decisions."

"Difficult situations are a chance to show your
strength and survive where no
one else thought you would."

"Opinion is not based on facts, so don't bother
yourself about other people's opinions."

"Every person is precious in their way,
they just don't appreciate themselves."

"It hurts to see black people destroying their
lives and hating those who build theirs."

"The secret to success is to be patient, relax.
Take your time and do things properly."

"Taking care of yourself is not an option,
it is a priority."

"Some people act like they
never do wrong."

"Being an introvert makes you see the
world for exactly what it is."

"Being black is hard, your people despise

you more than other races."

"Being black is hard, your people put a 100% effort
in making your life a nightmare."

"Peace of mind is a priceless
commodity."

"Material things don't define me,
I am devoted to being a better person each day."

"Despite all the insults and disrespect,
I am still improving my life."

"I always look back so I can get inspiration to get better."

"My downfalls have brought
my upbringing."

"Focusing on people and their issues
is a waste of your precious,
limited time on earth."

"We live only once, so do your best not
to regret a lot of bad decisions."

"I always try my best in everything that I do so I don't look back
and regret not taking advantage of the
opportunity that I had."

"I have learned from all the mistakes that I have made,
that is why
I will never make them again."

CHAPTER FIVE

"I only look back so I can get inspiration to get better."

"Just because you ill-treat me doesn't
mean I will change."

"Living is something that
we should all treasure."

"Great achievements require a
great amount of Time to be Invested."

"Just mind your own business and
you won't have time to judge others."

"Do the things that you love and
life won't just pass you by."

"My thoughts have helped me grow,
now I see everything for what it is."

"The more I think, the wiser I get."

"Don't pay any attention to people who disrespect you,
it doesn't make them
important people."

"Even if you don't have the support of people,
keep moving in the right direction."

"It doesn't matter who doesn't believe in you
as long as you believe in yourself."

"The things we take for granted: It's amazing how much
difference they make to other people's lives."

"The most important thing is being you and living
your life even if you don't have money"

"Don't put all your eggs in one basket,
you will live to regret it."

"As you grow up you find your true self."

"Never tell people that you have money,
you will live to regret it."

"Never change your plans for anybody."

"You must always preserve yourself
for a better tomorrow."

"Don't be busy judging other people,
live your life and let them judge you."

"I dedicate my life to doing what is right for me and my family."

"My peace of mind is my treasure."

"I am happy to be where I am, considering where I come from."

"My only regret in life is not being myself from the very beginning."

"Take time to perfect whatever it is you are doing, you won't regret it when you see the reward."

"The only person responsible for your happiness is you."

"The moment something doesn't feel right, stop right there."

"You only get wiser as you grow up."

"You only get wiser if you listen."

"Don't rush to make mistakes."

"Patience is key in every decision you make."

"Thinking too much makes me make the wrong decisions, I just need to do things."

"Improvement comes day by day, progress is necessary."

"Patience is the key to all success."

"Don't invest in something that will not benefit you in any way."

"I have learned to push my boundaries all the time. That is the only way I can fulfill my potential."

"I have decided not to worry about those that don't worry about me."

"I refuse to change regardless of your attitude towards me."

"Good people have taught me to always
seek what is good for me."

"Work on what you feel inside, the outside is always
victim to the crimes of the world."

"Work on yourself until you
know yourself."

"Every time you think you are
smart you are acting dumb."

"Every time I try to act smart,
I turn out to be dumber at the end."

"Life would be so simple if we just listen to each other."

"I have learned a lot from pain."

"People are good pretenders."

"I never want to look back at who I was, i
t's all about who I am now and who
I will be tomorrow."

"I don't have to be perfect,
I just need to keep improving."

"Taking time to do things will make them better."

"Patience is the key to doing
great things."

"Today is the most important day in
your life because you are still alive."

"The road to success is full of hard
work that nobody tells you about."

"Doing hard work when nobody is
watching is the key to success."

"Never pay attention to negative criticism,
people need to mind their own business."

"I don't know why people tell you
that you are not going to make it."

"Being in a rush will cost you dearly."

"Don't rush into making any decision,
some decisions affect you for the rest of your life."

"Love is so hard to find nowadays,
only material things matter."

"I appreciate all the blessings,
instead of complains"
"Always keep moving: that is the advice
I got from successful people."

"I learned not to pay attention to people who
are only interested in what they want."

"Some people only care about themselves,
but they want you to care about them."

"Greed never pays off."

"Never walk the same road twice,
the first time is a lesson."

"I look back with fondness when
I realize how much I have learned."

"The road to success is very steep,
you will need all your strength to make it."

"You will never see today ever again,
so cherish it."

"I miss the days when having fun
never involved alcohol."

"Your focus should be on more than one thing,
that way you will adapt and survive."

"Love will bring you happiness if
you expect nothing back."

"You can believe what you want,
I will remain who I am."

"It doesn't cost anything to be human."

"I always look forward to achieving
something new in my life."

"I promised myself that I wouldn't
die as a mediocre person."

"I was told that nobody is your friend,
people just use you until they get what they want."

"I never invest in something I
don't believe in."

"I keep to myself because no one has my
best interest at heart."

"I learned the hard way that
people are not to be trusted."

"Prioritize all the important things,
fun will come after."

"All moments are important,
don't regret taking them for granted."

"Cherish your life and all your blessings."

"Do your best in all things,
leave no regrets behind."

"Cheating will take you backwards,
you still don't understand anything."

"There are no shortcuts in life,
shortcuts are a recipe for disaster."

"The best lessons are learned the hard way."

"Learn to let go,
it is what is best for your heart."

"Despite all my setbacks,
I am still here and going strong."

"A lot of noise is not good,
quietness keeps me sane."

"The happier you are inside,
the more peace you will have."

"People judge you just because
you don't behave like them."

"Some people disrespect you just because
you don't agree with their point of view."

"Stop trying to be somebody
that you are not."

"I have never had loyal friends, a loyal girlfriend,
or loyal family.
So when I get money the last thing that comes to my mind

is marriage, parties, and family gatherings."

"You are hated for being unique."

"Being a good person hurts
but being a bad person is torture."

"Nobody is perfect so stop
judging and focus on yourself."

"I have never met a perfect human
being but some people are true morons"

"Patience is the key to all good things."

"At the end of the day,
you are living your life for yourself."

"No matter how much influence you get from outside,
only your decision matters at the end."

"You have no choice but to grow."

"Backstabbers teach you
about life and people."

"All people are two-faced,
it doesn't matter how good you are to them."

"Whether you show people respect or not,
they will remain who they are."

"Some people will never admit
when they are wrong."

"No matter how hard you try,
some people only care about themselves."

"Selfish people always want to
blame others for their faults."

"A woman will make you turn your back against
the world and then she will turn her back on you."

"People will make you ask yourself what you are
doing wrong every day only to find
out they are the real morons."

"I have learned a lot from people,
they will make your heart cold."

"A woman will do all she can to please you just so
that she can take everything that
you worked hard for."

"Listening to your heart instead of a woman is the best
decision you can make for
yourself and your family."

"Never give your all to a woman,
you will live to regret it forever."

"Always take advice that will work for you
and not the person who is giving you advice."

"Having a good time is
good for the soul."

"Even if someone annoys you, hate is not healthy for you."

"You lose yourself trying to please the world."

"Time helps you grow and become wiser and mature."

"In the blink of an eye, life changes."

"I didn't think that one day I would be
a responsible person but life has taught me harsh lessons."

"Life never goes
according to how we plan."

"A plan is just a structure to
get to a certain goal."

"I never forget how I started, it helps me
remember how I got here in the first place."

"I started with nothing,
I plan on ending with everything."

"I only look back with fondness
and smile as I realize how far I have come."

"I have no interest in seeing other people fail,
I am too focused on my life to
pay any attention."

"I look in the mirror and realize
I am not what you say I am, I am me."

"No matter how many times you disregard me,
I will keep being who I am."

"My time on earth is the only time I have left."

"I try my best to be the best that
I can be every single day"

"It has never been about how I look outside,
it has always been about who
I am when no one is looking."

"I wouldn't change the road that I
walked even if I had the chance."

"I never focus on what could have been,
I am more interested in what will be."

"I care about all humanity,
there is no point in hating people."

"I have nothing to gain by wishing
bad things on other people."

"We draw strength from
adversity."

"I have learned so many
lessons from pain."

"I have learned to love people
but never trust them."

"Living my life is the best thing
I have ever done for myself."

"Never live the life that others want for you,
live the one that makes you happy."

"No matter what the influence is,
remain true to who you are."

"I look forward to each day
because I only live once."

"Never trust a human being with everything."

"Let people do things for you and you
will learn how important it is to do it yourself."

"Life doesn't revolve around
certain situations, it's much bigger than that."

"Throughout my struggles,
I have learned that all shall pass one day."

"My behavior is a true
reflection of who I am."

"The true meaning of life is found when you
follow your heart and do what you love."

"My view of life is different from yours so
please don't try to change my views."

"Everywhere I walk,
I aim to leave a footprint of who I am."

"To all those that told me I would be nothing:
you see in others what you see in yourself."

"I am who I am, regardless of
what you say or think or do."

"Treat everyone with respect even
if they always disrespect you."

"People think you are crazy just because
you don't see life the way they see it."

"People want you to agree with their opinions so
they can justify whatever it is they want to say."

"I am true to myself."

"I remain faithful to who I am,
no matter how much it hurts."

"I live in a peaceful spirit,
no matter how much the world is against it."

"Try not to worry too much,
it's a disease."

"The fear of the unknown is
the fear to succeed."

"I am honored to be blessed
with the gift of writing."

"As long as life is moving
forward nothing else matters."

"You learn a lot from mistakes,
they make you a better human being."

"I always embrace my difficult situations,
they build me to be a stronger human being."

"Don't look back at all your faults,
there is nothing positive there."

"Never forget the reason you are
living in the first place."

"I miss being young,
I had no problems."

"Do your own thing, that way you won't
even notice what other people are up to."

"Life is a complicated journey,
don't complicate it even more."

"I embrace the difficulties of life,
it's an opportunity to prove how strong I am."

"Patience is the key to all success."

"No matter what life throws at me,
I will keep walking with my head held up high."

"I have been through worse than
what you can throw at me."

"I am stronger than all
your insults."

"All that matters is
what I believe in."

"Harsh lessons are
valuable life lessons."

"I will never change even if you can take
advantage of my kindness."

"I am who I am today because I never
changed when the world threw a storm at me."

"I will remain who I am no matter how
much disrespect you supply me with."

"I am happy to be who I am regardless
of how I am treated by others."

"If you are happy being you
then don't change."

"Being calm is good for
your health."

"Today is the day I am living for,
tomorrow is unknown."

"I always look forward to the next
challenge so that I can grow."

"I have long decided to let insults mean nothing to
who I am and who I will be in future."

"I will stay as I am until I die."

"Pain brings growth."

"I will let my work and actions speak
louder than my words."

"Don't ever wish to be someone else,
you will miss out on being you."

"My destiny will never be the same as yours so
don't waste your time trying to
follow another person."

"I have learned that trying is not enough,
I have to excel."

"My heart and soul belong to me
not the world."

"Everyone is in it for themselves,
that is the pure truth."

"I have experienced so much pain that life
doesn't surprise me anymore."

"I have learned to take care of myself first
because the world is a cold place."

"Living my life is a pleasure because
I don't try to be anyone else."

"I am forever trying to move on with my life,
with nothing holding me back."

"Good people are forever being hurt,
then we complain that there are too many morons in the world."

"Let life move right along and leave pessimistic
people behind where they belong."

"I always look forward to the next moment of my life,
I want to make my life an exciting journey."

"Work hard and let everything else
take care of itself."

"Growing up is something I treasure,
I am finally taking responsibility
for my life."

"Trying to impress people is a recipe for losing
yourself to the world."

"My life is a reflection of who I am"

"Mistakes help me grow from who I
was yesterday to who I am today."

"I take each day as it comes because
I have no idea where life is headed tomorrow."

"Keep moving because you don't know when the
train you are on will collapse."

"Keep on climbing the mountain,
you have no reason to stop."

"Loyalty to anyone or anything doesn't
pay unless if you are loyal to yourself."

"I had less stress as soon as I
decided to stop believing in lies."

"Don't believe everything you hear,
chances are it's far from the truth."

"Live your life on your terms then you
will truly know what happiness is."

"Finding yourself is the
best achievement."

"Life began when I decided
to stop existing and live."

"The greatest response
to an insult is silence."

"My life doesn't revolve around politics,
keep your issues to yourself."

"Life is much bigger than
our daily problems."

"The biggest barrier to
success is nepotism."

"Never assume you know
something that you don't know."

"It is better to learn than to
pretend like you know everything."

"Keep moving, time never s
tops to wait for you"

"Learn to move on quickly,
grief will slow you down."

CHAPTER SIX

"Spend time sharpening yourself in every way."

"Keep trying, that's all you can do."

"Don't try to be great,
just do your best."

"Make evolving a habit,
don't stop growing."

"Look back to learn
not to cry again."

"Insults don't deserve
your attention."

"Don't expect anything from people,
expect it from yourself."

"Angry people speak the truth,
believe everything they say."

"It's not about forgiving,
it's about peace of mind."

"Pain will teach you life lessons
you will never forget."

"Trusting people will prove why you
should never trust them."

"So much happens all at once,
get clarity."

"Life has been an interesting journey,
I look forward to more adventure."

"Take care of yourself,
that's all that matters."

"Look within,
you will find all that you seek."

"Believe in yourself,
no one else does."

"Support yourself,
no one else will."

"Follow your brain,
it's always logical."

"No one else is like you,

accept that and you will be at peace."

"Learn to live with yourself because
no one else will."

"Never put your heart and soul into
anything, only your brain."

"Don't jump to conclusions about anything,
check your facts."

"Keep moving in the right direction
despite all distractions."

"Life doesn't suck,
people make life suck."

"Tread carefully wherever you walk,
thorns only reveal themselves
when it's time to hurt you."

"Always be aware,
people take pride in your downfall."

"The life you live as young person
will result in the life you live as an elder."

"Give yourself a purpose,
it will make your life exciting."

"It's either you solve your problems or
other people's problems, you choose."

"What is right for you is not
necessarily what is right."

"Do what you think is right
not what you feel is right."

"Emotions always lead to
illogical decisions."

"Control your emotions otherwise
they will control you."

"What you say is not as
important as what you do."

"Take your time in making decisions
because there is no turning back."

"Learning patience is the hardest lesson
to teach yourself and to practice."

"In a world where everyone is in a hurry to do things,
your patience is very key
to your success in everything you do."

"Keep pushing boundaries."

"Your endurance will be tested all the time,
keep your stamina levels high."

"Keep motivating yourself,
no one else will."

"Self-reliance is the
best tool to possess."

"A purposeful life is a meaningful life."

"Setting goals will motivate you to wake up with energy."

"Never let anyone make decisions for you because you
will be left alone to face the
consequences of those decisions."

"Take responsibility for your life,
you are in charge."

"Self-motivation is the best motivation,
you don't have to wait for
someone to do it for you."

"Be comfortable being yourself,
it's the best feeling ever."

"The journey to finding yourself is full of obstacles,
keep moving forward."

"Today is the day I start working on myself,
not tomorrow."

"Life is a beautiful journey, just enjoy every moment."

Laugh more, you will find happiness

"Take each day as a blessing."

"Courage is the cornerstone of any man."

"Never give up on making something off your life, you have nothing to lose."

"Making the right decision takes heart, courage, and strength."

"There is no substitute for peace of mind."

"My actions define who I am, my words define what I believe."

"No man can ever take what I have
been blessed with."

"My life was not created to please people,
it was created to fulfill a purpose."

"Mother Nature created all people equally,
I'm not sure why other people act
like they are better than others."

"I am lucky that I am living my dream,
I hope you get a chance to live your dream too."

"I laugh because it is good for my soul not
because I want to look happy."

"There is no substitute
for peace of mind"

"Just because I don't broadcast my problems
doesn't mean I am living a nice life."

"Courage is the cornerstone
of any man."

"Life is precious,
that's all we need to know."

"Never give up on making something of your life,
you have nothing to lose."

"People judge without even
knowing the truth."

"Disappointment is part of my life,
maybe that's why I appreciate the joy when I find it."

"I am who I am because of what
I have been through."

"Life is not a fairytale, that's why you don't
always get what you want."

"Having friends is good for a person,
having true friends is a total blessing."

"I don't regret any decision that I make
because at the time it was the right decision."

"My actions define who I am,
my words define what I believe."

"My life has been defined by the
obstacles I have faced and overcome."

"Money doesn't define a person,
how he gets the money does."

"Time keeps moving, whether you are happy or sad.
So make the best out of it."

"Spend time doing the things
that make you happy."

"I have learned that people who don't know
you have a lot to say about you."

"I have grown up, not my body but
my mind, spirit and soul."

"Happiness doesn't exist in the world,
you have to create your own."

"It is an uphill road, its either you complain or
gather strength and reach the top."

"Tricky situations demand a
thoughtful process."

"Move swiftly, achieve all your
goals one at a time."

"Every challenge presents an opportunity to
prove you are a worthy adversary."

"Talent takes you to the promised land but talent
combined with hard work will keep you there."

"
Have patience,
impatience is for the weak-minded."

"Take every moment as it comes,
don't be in a rush to go anywhere."

"Be a student in everything, there will never come a
day where you know everything

about everything."

"Constant improvement is a recipe
for constant success."

"Your past paved the way for today and today
will pave a way for your future."

"You are wiser than your problems."

"Solutions are always there,
all you need to think."

"Think bigger than your problems and you
will always have a solution."

"Ask if you don't know,
ignorance will never lead you to success."

"Never promise anyone anything,
you don't know what tomorrow will bring."

"Trust must be reserved
for one person, yourself."

"Don't ever try to impress
people, nobody cares."

"Keep your things to yourself otherwise
they shall be ripped away from you."

"Be careful who you seek advice from,
some people will contribute to
your downfall instead of helping your rise."

"Don't depend on anyone,
you are likely to regret it."

"Success breeds success."

"Failure breeds lessons to use to succeed."

"Manage your fears,

not every opportunity is to be feared."

"Teach yourself the value of self-love,
no one will love you as you love yourself."

"Once you compromise one belief,

you will compromise all the others because it
will quickly become a habit."

The habit of reading breeds success."

I am built to withstand a tsunami because those who
have taught me defeated the
tsunami that was against them."

The storm comes and goes, just hold your ground for a
little while and you will
be sorted for life."

"Don't stop anyone's progress,
instead, progress together."

"Love yourself enough
not to hate others."

"Love yourself more
than you hate others."

"Respect yourself so
you can respect others."

"Take care of yourself,
it's the only time you will be alive."

"Teach yourself self-love, it's
vital to your longevity."

"Bring comfort to your heart,
only you can do it."

"The time to be yourself is now."

"Keep your desire burning,
it's the only way for constant improvement."

"Stay away from negative
environments."

"Stay away from toxic people,
they will poison you."

"Helping each other grow is easier
than destroying each other."

"A little step in the right direction is better
than a big step in the wrong direction."

"A positive spirit never dies,

it is re-born all the time."

"Spiting on others damages you
emotionally and mentally."

"Don't lose focus of what is
important to you, ever."

"It's better to be a step ahead than to
be a step behind, keep moving."

"Don't compromise your beliefs,
you won't recognize yourself."

"Don't stop the hustle,
stop the excuses"

"You need the right mindset to channel
your focus on what you are doing."

"It doesn't matter what happens,
nobody can take away all that you have achieved."

"Don't listen to untalented,
stupid people who have never achieved anything."

"Don't take advice from anyone
who has never achieved anything."

"Do everything you want not
everything everybody wants."

"No honesty lives in this world,
just lies, and agendas."

"The true essence of life is to
live life on your terms."

"Keep doing good things,
especially for yourself."

"You can never go wrong
with a little kindness."

"Despite all obstacles,
just keep moving."

"Don't stop because there is a distraction,
work through it."

"Make the best of your time,
you will never get it back."

CHAPTER SEVEN

"Don't compromise your future for a few seconds of fun and gratification."

"Your time is precious, use it wisely."

"Don't waste your time on fruitless conversations with people who lack ambition and knowledge."

"The biggest waste of your time is gossip."

"Nothing drains you like negative people."

"Reserve your energy for important tasks."

"Don't worry about people, they are not worried about you."

"Don't do anything you don't want to do, you will regret it."

"Follow your journey, solve your problems, live your own life."

"Think ahead, though you are alive today, you will still be alive ten years from now."

"Take care of your dreams and they will take care of you."

"Every step you take will determine where you will be in the future."

"Don't be afraid to take a risk, life is a risk, after all, anything can happen at anytime."

"The little effort you put in will make a big difference to the bigger picture."

"Measure your progress, that way you can revitalize your energy to improve."

"Inspire yourself before you are inspired by others."

"The motivation you give yourself is more important than the motivation you get from others."

"Open your ears and eyes and learn."

"Your mouth will either destroy you or build you."

"Don't focus on anything that you won't benefit from."

"Whatever little you have, be grateful,
it's better than having nothing at all."

"No one can ever take away
your talent and skill."

"Don't aim to destroy,
aim to empower."

"Embrace change, don't fight it."

"Embrace talent, don't hate it."

"Don't try to control everything,
let things be."

"Don't look back,
nothing matters back there."

"The ability to improve
all the time is a gift."

"Take note of your struggles,
they build you."

"Don't pay attention to anything
that doesn't matter to you."

"Tread carefully,
not everybody wants you to win"

"Don't think about anything
else except your progress."

"One step each day is better
than doing nothing."

"Opinions won't help you
achieve anything."

"Your actions will determine
your success rate."

"The only reasonable action is to
keep moving forward."

"True character is shown when you are
surrounded by people who are different."

"Take charge of your life, no one else will."

"Your main focus is yourself, above anything else."

"Always reflect on all your decisions so
you can do better next time."

"Tomorrow is another day to do
better than you did today."

"What you don't know now,
you can learn and know it today."

"Don't postpone anything,
right now is the right time."

"Don't ask for support from people
who know you, you will never get it."

"Take a step in the right direction every day,
don't wait for anything."

"Love yourself more than you love others."

"Improve your craft all the time so
you can be successful all the time."

"What I have learned can never be taken away from me."

"No matter what happens,
you can't diminish my light."

"There is nothing wrong with dedication
and commitment to yourself."

"Dedication and commitment to
your dreams is vital."

"Only pay attention to your dreams,
don't live other people's dreams."

"Don't trade your soul for anything."

"Keep your soul to yourself."

"Grow your love, not your hate."

"Hatred is a waste of time, worrying about people
that don't worry about you."

"Insults are an indication that you are
doing something right for you."

"You can't make everyone happy,
hence some people will never like you."

"Move along swiftly, don't ever stop."

"Don't ever talk about people,
you are wasting time you will never get back."

"Don't focus on your flaws,
focus on your strengths, they will build you."

"Keep working,
only success will come from working hard."

"Get to action as soon as you can."

"Have gratitude, it's the only way to maintain your success."

"If you are waiting for support from family and friends, you will wait forever."

"The courage to take your path is true strength
"Master yourself."

"Know yourself more
than you know others."

"Your emotions won't contribute to
your success but your downfall."

"Kill laziness otherwise,
it will kill your dreams."

"The action you take today will determine your
success tomorrow so don't procrastinate."

"Don't listen to anyone who hasn't
achieved the success you seek."

"Don't express your opinion about
everything, it doesn't matter."

"The less you expect from people the
less you will be disappointed."

"Expectation will lead you to
major disappointment."

"The truth will relieve you
of any false beliefs."

"Don't judge people, there is no time for that."

"Don't waste your time, you can't change the world."

"Only you can uplift yourself."

"Give yourself a chance,
you can be successful if you put 110% into it."

"Believe that it can happen and it will."

"Start the process of being successful,
what are you waiting for."

"Continue pushing yourself,
you are almost there."

"It doesn't matter what happens,
all that matters is that you are still alive."

"Hold on to what you have,
the world only wants to take it away from you."

"Don't lie to yourself,
no one is on your side."

"I will keep doing me,
it doesn't matter how many people are against me."

'Don't fight against opposing opinions,
they are useless.'

"Complement yourself on
your achievements."

"Don't ever depend on anyone,
there is no guarantee that they will be there."

"The greatest weapon you
can take into the war of life is you."

"Treasure your talent,
it is your ticket to a bright future."

"Study yourself as you study others."

"Monitor your strengths,
they are vital to your growth."

"Calm down, losing your temper
won't solve the problem."

"Wait for the right time to make a move, speed kills."

"For your dreams to come true,
move past the obstacles."

"Bravery is good as long as you
are not risking your life."

"Take responsibility for the
situations you put yourself in."

"Take responsibility for fixing
yourself and your life."

"Tackle one obstacle and get through it,
that is the process for success."

"Know your best qualities and you
can use them to uplift yourself."

"Before you worry about others,
worry about yourself."

"Before you care about others,
care about yourself."

"Forget hateful people,
they are not important."

"Stay away from people who talk
too much, that's all they do."

"From the beginning till the end,
we keep working."

"All that I have learned can never
be taken away from me."

"It's never too late to start
working on yourself."

"Don't think about the useless people who
never contributed anything to your life."

"Don't believe those who don't believe in you."

CHAPTER EIGHT

"Believe in your dreams and they
will believe in you."

"Why are people worried about what you
do instead of what they do?."

"The moment you take things into your own hands is
the moment your life will change for the better."

"It doesn't matter how
much you hate me."

"Question everything and you will learn
more than you ever imagined."

"Don't forget who you truly are."

"Try new things,
it will refresh your mind."

"Always convince yourself that
you are good enough."

"Try your best,
that's all you can do."

Never try to fit in
anywhere."

"By trying to fit in, it means
you don't belong there."

"Try not to fall while you uplift others."

"Don't change your plans,
adjust your plans."

"There is nothing wrong with taking a step back,
rushing never solved anything."

"Give nothing away,
the less people know about you the better."

"The life you live is yours, take care of it."

"Don't be afraid to start again."

"Take each day as it comes,
don't be afraid to make slow progress."

"Some people have no interest in seeing you prosper,
watch out for them."

"Some people want you to be nothing with them."

"I don't know everything,
that's why I learn every day."

"I miss being young,
nobody had issues with me."

"Your inner peace makes those at
war with themselves angry at you."

"Dig down inside so you
can proper outside."

"March forward in the belief that
everything will be alright."

"Stay on course, whether it
rains or there is sunshine."

"I still believe in myself,
whether you ridicule me or not."

"I will hold my head up high regardless
of the way you ill-treat me."

"I was created by nature not by a deity."

"Be open to change,
it will change your life."

"I didn't give up, that's
why I'm here today."

"To be sane you need to
stay in your lane."

"Nothing can hold you back except the
negative thoughts on your mind."

"Trying to please the world is a
recipe for disaster."

"You can't solve everyone's problems."

"Never assume anything,
figure it out first."

"Conclusions are the
root of evil."

"It's either you are going in the right direction or the
wrong direction, there is no middle ground."

"True character is found during adversity."

"True knowledge is knowing thyself."

"Stay out of your comfort zone,
always."

"If you want to grow,
make your comfort zone your enemy."

"Experience is the true cornerstone
of wisdom."

"Keep believing,
things will happen for you."

"Keep the positivity, your dreams will come true."

"Don't ever stop believing in yourself
regardless of what the rest of the world believes."

"Support is the
best form of love."

"Don't forget to support the
people who need it."

"Your kindness might brighten
someone's bad day."

"Don't be ashamed to be
nice in a cruel world."

"Don't waste your energy on
unimportant matters."

"Every second counts, don't wait till you
are old to realize this."

"Push your work, that's all that matters."

"Stay true to yourself,
you won't regret it."

"Stay out of matters that have
nothing to do with you."

"Peace is minding your
own business."

"The joy of silence is more precious
than you can ever imagine."

"Don't do things because others
are doing them."

"Keep your distance from negativity,
it will do the same for you."

"Move silently, that way, whoever wants to
sabotage you won't know what to sabotage."

"Be careful, there are too many
snakes behind a lot of smiles."

"There is no honor,
only deceit in the world we live in today."

"Treat yourself gently,
nobody else will."

"The only person who will love you
more than everybody is you."

"True genius lies in knowing that
you must grow every day."

"The problem with not believing in yourself is
the opinions you listen to."

"Opinions have never made
anyone successful."

"True champions don't value the
opinions of unsuccessful people."

"Steady growth is always better
than overnight success, it lasts."

"Open your mind, ears, and eyes.
On the other side,
you will find success in everything you do."

"Maybe the true motivation is knowing there
is nothing to be gained by giving up."

"Despite public opinion,
you have nothing to prove to anyone."

"Doubt is not self-imposed,
it is imposed by public opinions."

"Influence is the biggest
part of decision making in society."

"If you truly love yourself, no one can convince
you to treat yourself with disdain."

"Pull together all your strengths
and you will thrive."

"Don't focus on your weaknesses,
they will mess up your self-esteem."

"Look inside for inspiration."

"Inspire yourself to do
better all the time."

"After all is said and done,
only you can make things happen for yourself."

"Working with like-minded people is a
joy in itself."

"Take care of every aspect
of your life."

"Try new things,
it's a great feeling."

"Groom yourself to be the
best version of yourself."

"Learning brings me tranquility,
knowing that I am growing with
each ounce of knowledge."

"Taking responsibility for every part of my
life was a choice that I
made for myself."

"Take it slow, don't rush anything."

"Everything must be done
properly when the time is right."

"Never compromise yourself for anyone,
you will regret it."

"What is life to you?
That is all that matters"

"Step away from everything that
doesn't make you happy."

"Too much noise clouds your clarity."

"Avoid distractions, they will stop you
from achieving your goals."

"Everyone is just pushing their agenda,
just do your own thing."

"Nobody cares about what you want,
push your hustle."

"Your growth is subject to how much motivation
you have to be a better
human being."

"There is no permanent state of mind
unless you refuse to
open your mind."

"Sleep and wake up feeling better."

"Everywhere you go, everyone is trying to turn you into something you are not"

"As I grow older, people don't change, they just keep using the same bullying tactics"

"Critics only have big mouths and no achievements"

"Everyone is a good talker except when it's time to talk about their achievements"

"You must learn something valuable from every encounter"

"Search for the truth in everything that is meant to put you down"

"Never walk in the footsteps of others otherwise your identity fades"

"Work, Work, Work, Rest and then do more Work"

"Write your name in folk-law, don't worry about anything else"

"There is no clear path to success"

"Learn to deal with obstacles, for they always find a way into your life"

"Do something, it's the only way to move forward"

"Take your time, life is not a race"

"Criticism comes from those who spend their time thinking about how to put down others"

"Don't waste your time on anything, you will never get it back"

"Everybody is always trying to change you, trying to create a duplicate of themselves"

"The more I stay original and authentic, the more effort is made to change me into another copy of something everyone is"

"Don't explain yourself, you are wasting your energy"

"Start walking to where you want to go, NOW"

"Unique qualities are the start of your renaissance"

"The negativity they throw your way should be the fuel you need to be positive"

"Negative energy is the energy needed to realize you only need positive thoughts in your life"

"Never let peasants dictate the way a King should live his life, there is a reason they are peasants"

"Adversity is overcome with consistent positivity"

"The life you live is a reflection of how much you value yourself"

"You can never kill my spirit, no matter how hard you try"

"The effort you put in trying to put down others should be the effort you put in to make your dreams a reality"

"True inspiration comes from knowing that nothing can put you down"

"Whether people believe in you or not, that will never determine your success"

"The time you spend worrying about opinions is the time you must spend honing your craft"

"The less opinions you listen to the greater your success will be"

"Be fearful of stupidity, that is how you become nobody"

"Don't try to stay relevant, stay foolish"

"Your life story is your truth"

"So many doubters who are reading this quote, I guess your doubts are useless"

"Don't waste your energy on useless activities like pleasing people"

"Your heart is yours, hence it's called your heart. Why are you giving it to others?"

"Your brain will either be your meal ticket or lead you to poverty"

"Everything comes and goes except your morals"

"True character is defined by standing on your two feet regardless of how strong the wind is blowing"
"I have stood my ground despite all stones that were thrown in my direction"

"The reason I am still standing is because I am rooted in my truth"

"Try silence, you will discover the magic of intelligence"

"A silent human being realizes how that noise is a waste of time"

"Remind yourself that only worthless people have time to attack valuable people"

"Even in sports, commentators watch others achieve greatness"

"Don't bark like a dog, roar like a lion"

"The best way to move forward is to keep doing what you do best"

"Your true character is not determined by gossip and rumours"

"Nobody can take away your talent, Nobody"

"Keep the fire in your soul burning"

"Try action, forget procrastination"

"The day I moved in the right direction I became a source of hatred for those who enjoyed my failure"

"I climbed the mountain thinking everyone was cheering for my victory but instead, they were cheering for my downfall"

"Don't worry about those who don't believe in you, they don't even believe in themselves"

"Don't spend time with opinionated people, their greatest achievement is expressing a billion opinions"

"Don't start listening to anyone who doesn't listen to himself/herself when he/she speaks"

"The reason people even notice you is because there is something good about what you are doing"

"I walk, they talk"

"Why would I wish anything bad on you? I won't gain anything"

"I kept myself inspired despite adversity"

"I stayed on course to achieve my goals, what have you done?"

"I promise to never talk about you, I don't have time to waste"

"Take the right path for yourself"

"Step forward, for this is the only chance you have"

"Your soul belongs to you, only you"

"My backbone is like steel, trying to break it is a waste of time"

"They did all they could to destroy me, unfortunately they didn't know the depth of my character"

"As I walk in my truth, nothing can shake me, even death"

"Your attempt to hurt me is proof that I am doing something right"

"No matter how many stones you throw, I am not a glass house"

"I am made of steel, your hatred can't shake my resolve"

"Although the wind blows in all directions, you will find me rooted to my core beliefs"

"Looking back at all the insults, none of them changed my belief in my ability to excel"

"As a black man, my adversity is my skin colour and the people who look like me"

"I have never doubted myself, and I won't start now"

"I put all my energy into achieving my dreams, whether you believe in me or not"

"As usual, all you are interested in is trying to make me feel worthless just like you"

"The feeling of achieving your dreams without paying attention to nay-sayers is the key to true success"

"Talented people don't pay attention to untalented people. It's always the other way around"

"You will always get stinking attitude from people who are bitter about being untalented, as if it's your fault"

"Your hatred won't define whether I'm successful or not"

"Move forward at all costs, no matter what stands in your way"

"People will always go out of their way to make you feel crazy for being talented"

"Don't wake up thinking of anything but your dreams"

"The less said, the better for everyone"

"I read that reading is a tool for success"

"Don't talk about people, gossip is for people with empty lives and an empty existence"

"Give yourself time to succeed, you need it"

"Although there was no motivation from anyone, I found motivation in myself and reached levels I never thought were possible"

"Stay true to your core values, without them, you have nothing"

"Don't move mountains for anyone, they won't even move a pen for you"

"Don't challenge a hungry lion, wait till he has a full stomach and reeks of complacency and arrogance"

"Feed an ego so the ego can lead to his/her downfall"

"The truth of the matter is: Your opinion doesn't matter"

"The real reason you want to talk is because nobody cares"

"I keep myself busy, being idle leads to decay"

"If you were important, you wouldn't have to prove it, at all"

"As soon as you find yourself, you reach a level of tranquillity that money can't pay for"

"I never understood my surroundings, only when I understood myself"

"To believe that you are correct even though people are against you is true self-belief"

"Don't honour love, honour family, honour the truth and honour yourself"

"It doesn't matter what has been taken away from me, you can't take away my talent and my wisdom"

"I am laser focused on my goals, you need to let me be"

"You can't destabilise true genius, you can only destabilise stupidity"

"My word is my bond, for my truth lies in what I say"

"I don't believe anything you say about me, you only know what you think you know"
"My time is not up for sale, I don't sell hours for respect"

"Desperation for attention calls for stupid people to have opinions on everything"

"Don't believe the hype, only success will make you relevant"

"I have learned that learning doesn't stop"

"Don't stop your growth"

"Live to improve"

"Stay true to yourself, you are all you've got"

"A move in the right direction is never wrong"

"Don't think too much, you will procrastinate"

"The more I work hard, the more luck I get"

"It's all the obstacles I face that strengthen me"

"I will keep walking, in spite of you"

"Moving a step closer is better than moving backwards"

"Keep yourself warm, no one else will"

"Never hesitate to do what is best for you"

"By growing, you help those around you grow"

"Your life story shouldn't be filled with any other story except yours"

"Contrary to popular belief, money actually defines you"

"As I grow older, I realized I have wasted so much time on useless things"

"Stay Positive, Stay Active"

"Hold yourself responsible for your life, you won't regret it"

"Don't lose sleep over things you can't control"

"You can't control everything, relax"

"Learn to pick your battles, too much noise pollutes the mind"

"Don't fight, silence is better"

"Sometimes there is no need to win an argument, stay silent and find peace"

"I still don' understand hatred, what do you get for it?"

"If hatred made people rich, 98% of the population would be wealthy"

"Take action on all the knowledge you acquire"

"Think good thoughts, they are healthy"

"Keep track of your goals so you can measure your progress"

"Persevere, no matter what"

"People only want to talk about themselves, let them"

"Do you but don't get angry when others do the same"

"Treat each day with respect, don't waste your precious time on earth"

"Focus, distraction or not, focus"

"Happiness is doing what you want not what people think will make you happy"

"I'm grateful for all the lies in the world, now I know the truth"

"Commenting on anything and everything is a total waste of energy"

"Reserve your energy for the most important stuff in your life"

"I am me, not because of arrogance but because I am rooted in my beliefs"

"The family you have is all you have"

"Today I am a better person because I picked up a book"

"I believe in me, not because others believe but because I have to believe"

"I never stopped believing, hence I'm here"

"Try your best, it's better than doing nothing"

"Don't waste your time trying to understand others, spend your time understanding yourself"

"Let's encourage each other to reach our dreams"

"Why work so hard to ruin other people's lives?"

"Your enthusiasm shouldn't be ruined by negative vibes"

"Don't stay in one place for too long, habits are hard to break"

"The state of your mind shouldn't be determined by what others do"

"What you believe might not necessarily be the truth"

"Once you start improving, don't ever stop"

"Take note of what drunk people say, they speak nothing but the truth"

"Alcohol reveals people's true feelings and thoughts"

"Nobody says anything by mistake, they mean it"

"Improve at your own pace, life is not a race but a journey"

"Seek tranquillity, there is too much noise in the world"

"Stay away from chaos, it denies you clarity"

"Stay connected to your soul, don't sell it to anyone"

"Stand your ground, whatever storm may come"

"I accept who I am, I deflect who I am not"

"You probably don't like me, I probably don't care"

"Pursue what you desire, it's not a crime"

"Don't waste your time on futile exercises
like trying to get people to like you"

"Trying to impress people is like trying to be someone you are not,
you will never win"

"Truthfully speaking, your fake friends
will never help you succeed"

"Tons of criticism and no support, s
ounds like the journey of a black man"

"Pay attention to how people react when you do something nice for yourself,
the truth will reveal itself"

"The biggest lie in the world: I love you unconditionally"

"The true meaning of hatred is envy"

"The depth of your hatred won't
make me unsuccessful"

"Your lack of support won't determine my success"

"After meeting so many negative people,
you realize their opinions don't matter"

"You are only stressing yourself by
thinking of people that don't matter"

"Never regret helping people, there is nothing you did wrong"

"Try moving forward, there is
nothing but baggage behind you"

"Only by exploring new avenues do we grow"

"There is nothing interesting behind you, your future awaits"

"Patience, it takes years to hone any craft"

"One step each day is all it takes to reach the promised-land"

"Keep believing, support or no support"

"Fight till there is nothing
left and then fight even more"

"The storm comes in unexpected ways,
I will fight back in unexpected ways"

"When the storms begins, I roll up my sleeves"

"Through my struggles, I grow"

"Through my pain, I become stronger than before"

"Through my mistakes, I learn"
"Failure is not my obstacle, it is my opportunity to learn to do better"

"True strength lies in fighting relevant battles"

"Find humility in your true self"

"Happiness is a meal you have to cook
and dish up for yourself"

"What is outside won't bring you peace inside"

"Our beliefs do not necessarily reflect reality"

"You are mocked before success,
sabotaged when you achieve success and they rejoice in your downfall.
You are on your own"

"The hard work you put in before success is forgotten
when you are successful, as if you woke up one day and became the
president of the country without doing anything"

"You don't matter when you have nothing to give"

"They are only interesting because they see something
to benefit from an association with you"

"Know the difference between true friends,
material friends, leeches and bloodsuckers"

"Treat your loyal friends gently, everybody else doesn't care about you"

"Speak properly,
you can never take back your words"

"Be gentle to your soul,
it has endured a lot"

"Stop criticizing, start working on your own deficiencies"

"Stop analysing what's wrong with
others but rather what's wrong with you"

"There is no growth in pointing fingers"

"You never move forward because you are
always worried about what happened before"

"Anxiety about the past is a recipe for future failure"

"Start right away,
only now matters"

"Finding yourself is the only
journey that matters"

"Move away and focus on yourself"

"Healing comes from taking responsibility"

"Fresh air is required to refresh the mind and body"

ABOUT THE AUTHOR

My name is Sibusiso Kumalo. I was born at Chris Hani Baragwanath Hospital on the 1st of August 1986. Then I stayed with my mother, father and older sister at Mofolo before we moved to Doornkop, Roodepoort (previously under Soweto). I attended grade 1-3 at Vuyolwethu Primary School then attended grade 4-7 at Hector Pietersen Primary school in Dobsonville Ext 3. I attended Grade 8 at Kwadedangendlala High School in Zola then attended grade 9-12 at R.W. Fick High School in Bosmont.
I dropped out of various tertiary courses, Business management (after one year). Web Design (I didn't write the final exam). As well as another Business course (only did six months).
When I was young I played a lot of sports, soccer, cricket and even athletics. I represented my primary school until I went to high school. When I got to high I only played till grade 9 and then I decided to stop and focus on my studies because they were subpar. That decision led to an increase in pass rate and decrease in my sporting activities. I did well from grade 10-11 but my life drastically changed in grade 12.

Instead of focusing on my studies I developed habits that took me away from what matters the most, focusing on my future and career. I fell in love with music, Kwaito, R 'n B, Hip-Hop and a bit of Gospel. I decided to stop focusing on my school work and focus on building a music career. That ambition didn't last long as I am a person who loses interest easily. When I was 11 I went for trials at Orlando Pirates FC, a big football club from Soweto. I passed my initial trial and got called up to attend a trial session with the actual under-12 Orlando Pirates team. As a young person, I didn't take it seriously. I didn't go. When I was 13 I went to cricket trials for the Gauteng cricket franchise. I got selected to come and continue the trial with the actual under-15 team but again, I didn't go. I lost interest in being a sports superstar as I lost interest in being a musician.
I have tried out a lot of things in terms of work but they all didn't work out. One day in 2007 when I was supposed to meet up with someone a friend suggested that I come and see a rehearsal session where he was training young actors in Dapp Centre in Doornkop, Roodepoort. As soon as I saw what they were doing, I fell in love with Theatre work. I tried out for acting but realized it's not my thing as I am too shy to appear on TV or even speak in front of people. Then again, a friend suggested that maybe I can write a story. I met up with someone who turned out to be my longtime friend, Sibusiso "Mababa" Ntuli. We co-wrote a story called My Kasie Story, although nothing materialised from it, that's when I realized that I can do this for the rest of my life. This was in 2009 and from that day on I never looked back.

Today I am the author of my very first book, LESSONS LEARNT.
I am a TV and FILM writer and director. I have done work on these various shows: Bone Of My Bones; Mzali Wam'; Isidingo; HouseMaids; HouseWives; Ikhaya Labadala and currently on Lingashoni.

www.ingramcontent.com/pod-product-compliance
Lightning Source LLC
Chambersburg PA
CBHW021019090426
42738CB00007B/831